Practical Guide to the Operational Use of the HK MP5 Submachine Gun, 9x19mm

Erik Lawrence
erik@vig-sec.com

Printed and bound in the United States of America

First printing 2015

ISBN-13: 978-1-941998-78-6
EBOOK ISBN: 978-1-941998-79-3

ATTENTION US MILITARY UNITS, US GOVERNMENT AGENCIES AND PROFESSIONAL ORGANIZATIONS: Quantity discounts are available on bulk purchases of this book. Special books or book excerpts can also be created to fit specific needs. For information, please contact:

Erik Lawrence
erik@vig-sec.com

Firearms are potentially dangerous and must be handled responsibly by individuals. The technical information presented in this manual on the use of the MP5 Submachine Gun reflects the author's research, beliefs, and experiences. The information in this book is presented for academic study only. Neither the author nor the publisher assumes any responsibility for the use or misuse of information contained in this book.

SAFETY NOTICE
Before starting an inspection, ensure the weapon is cleared. Do not manipulate the trigger until the weapon has been cleared of all ammunition. Inspect the chamber to ensure that it is empty and no ammunition is present. Keep the weapon oriented in a safe direction when loading and handling.

AMMUNITION NOTICE- This weapon fires several different calibers, so be sure you know which model of model you are using and match the ammunition accordingly. Firing the incorrect ammunition will damage the weapon and possibly injure the operator.

Training should be received from knowledgeable and experienced operators on this particular weapons system. Vigilant Security Services Training provides this training and continually perfects its instruction with up-to-date information from actual use.

www.vig-sec.com

Table of Contents

Section 1 1

Introduction 1

Description 2

Background 4

Trigger Group Options 6

Safety Operation 7

Variants 12

Section 2 23

Maintenance 23

Clearing the MP5 SMG 25

Disassembling the MP5 SMG 27

Reassembling the MP5 SMG 31

Performing a Function Check on the MP5 SMG 34

Maintenance of the Magazine 35

Section 3 36

Operation and Function 36

Cycle of Function 36

Loading the MP5 Magazine 36

Loading the Magazine into a MP5 SMG 37

Firing the MP5 SMG 39

Section 4 40

Performance Problems 40

Malfunction and Immediate Action Procedures 40

Section 1

Introduction

The objective of this manual is to allow the reader to be able to use the variants of Heckler and Koch (HK) designed MP5 submachine guns (SMG) competently. The manual will give the reader background on/specifications of the weapon; instructions on its operation, disassembly, and assembly; proper firing procedure; and malfunction/misfire procedures. Operator-level maintenance will also be detailed to allow the reader to understand and become competent in the use and maintenance of the MP5 SMG variants.

Figure 1-1 MP5N

Figure 1-2 MP5A2

Description

The MP5 Submachine Gun

The characteristics of the HK MP5 SMG:

A. Country of Origin: Germany

B. Military Designation: MP5 (with identifier codes)

C. Operation: Full, burst, and/or semi-automatic fire

D. Cartridge: 9x19mm, 10mm, .40 S&W

E. Length: See below for variations

    a. Fixed stock:

- 26.7 in./680 mm (MP5A2, MP5A4, MP5/10, MP5/40)

- 31 in./790 mm (MP5SD2, MP5SD5)

    b. Telescoping stock:

- 27.6 in./700mm with stock extended/21.7 in./550mm with stock collapsed (MP5A3, MP5A5)
- 23.7 in./603mm with stock extended/14.5 in./368mm with stock folded (MP5K-PDW)
- 31.7 in./805mm with stock extended/36.4 in./670mm with stock collapsed (MP5SD3, MP5SD6)
- 26 in./660mm with stock extended/19.3 in./490mm with stock collapsed (MP5/10, MP5/40)

    c. Receiver end cap:

- 12.9 in./325mm (MP5K, MP5KA1, MP5KA4, MP5KA5)
- 13.7 in./349mm (MP5K-PDW)
- 21.7 in./550mm (MP5SD1, MP5SD4)

F. Barrel: See below for variations, right-hand twist

    a. 8.8 in./225 mm (MP5A2, MP5A4, MP5A3, MP5A5, MP5/10, MP5/40)
    b. 5.5 in./140 mm (MP5K-PDW)
    c. 5.8 in./146 mm (MP5SD1, MP5SD4, MP5SD2, MP5SD5, MP5SD3, MP5SD6) Width 50 mm (MP5A2, MP5A4, MP5A3, MP5A5, MP5K, MP5KA1, MP5KA4, MP5KA5, MP5K-PDW, MP5/10, MP5/40)
    d. 8.3 in./210 mm (MP5K, MP5KA1, MP5KA4, MP5KA5, MP5K-PDW)

G. Weight: See below for variations

    a. 5.6 lbs./2.54 kg (MP5A2, MP5A4)
    b. 6.8 lbs./3.08 kg (MP5A3, MP5A5)
    c. 4.4 lbs./2.00 kg (MP5K, MP5KA1, MP5KA4, MP5KA5)
    d. 6.1 lbs./2.78 kg (MP5K-PDW)

  e. 6.2 lbs./2.80 kg (MP5SD1, MP5SD4)
  f. 6.8 lbs./3.10 kg (MP5SD2, MP5SD5)
  g. 8 lbs./3.60 kg (MP5SD3, MP5SD6)
  h. 5.9 lbs./2.67 kg with fixed stock 6 lbs./2.85 kg with folding stock (MP5/10)
  i. 5.9 lbs./2.67 kg with fixed stock 6 lbs./2.85 kg with folding stock (MP5/40)

H. Type of Feed: 15-, 30-, or 40-round detachable box

I. Operating System: Roller-delayed blowback, closed bolt

J. Rate of Fire:
  a. 800 rounds/min (MP5A2, MP5A4, MP5A3, MP5A5, MP5SD1, MP5SD4, MP5SD2, MP5SD5, MP5SD3, MP5SD6)
  b. 900 rounds/min (MP5K, MP5KA1, MP5KA4, MP5KA5, MP5K-PDW)

K. Maximum Effective Range: 200 meters

L. Muzzle Velocity:
  a. 1312 fps/400 m/s (MP5A2, MP5A4, MP5A3, MP5A5)
  b. 1230 fps/375 m/s (MP5K, MP5KA1, MP5KA4, MP5KA5, MP5K-PDW)
  c. 935 fps/285 m/s (MP5SD1, MP5SD4, MP5SD2, MP5SD5, MP5SD3, MP5SD6)
  d. 1394 fps/425 m/s (MP5/10)
  e. 1033 fps/315 m/s (MP5/40)

Background

Founded by Edmond Heckler, Alex Seidel and Theodore Koch, all former Mauser Werke employees, H&K commenced operations in 1948 in Oberndorf/Neckar as a manufacturer of sewing machine parts and gauges for the machine tool industry.

The MP5 (short for *Maschinenpistole* 5) was created within the fourth group of firearms, initially known as the **HK54**.

Design

The **MP5** began as a 9x19mm submachine gun of German design, developed in the 1960s by a group of engineers from the West German arms manufacturer Heckler & Koch GmbH (HK). The company, motivated by the success of the G3 rifle, developed a group of small arms consisting of four types of firearms (all based on the G3 design layout), where the first type was chambered in 7.62x 51 mm NATO rifle cartridge, the second used the 7.62x39 mm M43 round, the third used the intermediate 5.56x45 mm NATO caliber and the fourth type – chambered the 9x19 mm Parabellum pistol cartridge.

The most salient feature of H&K's line of small arms is the roller-delayed blowback, roller-locking system of operation. This method of operation first appeared in the StG 45M developed at the Mauser Werke in 1945. It was part of the continuing evolution of the assault rifle concept initiated by the MP 44.

The Heckler & Koch system weapons operate as follows: The bolt mechanism consists of two major components, the bolt head and the bolt carrier. Although referred to as locking rollers, the action is never totally locked. In the firing position, inclined surfaces on the locking piece within the bolt carrier lie between the two rollers on the bolt head and force them out into recesses in the barrel extension. After ignition, the rollers are cammed inward against the locking piece's inclined planes by rearward pressure on the bolt head. The bolt carrier's rearward velocity is four times that of the bolt head. After the bolt carrier has moved rearward 4mm, the rollers on the bolt head (which has moved only 1 mm) are completely in, pressure has dropped to the required levels of safety, and the two parts continue their backward movement together. Several years ago, the MP5 bolt head was improved and strengthened to inhibit cracking. Unbeknownst to most, the MP5 bolt carrier contains 32.5 grams of tungsten granules, which serve as an anti-bounce device.

The first submachine gun based on this method of operation appeared in the early 1960s and was called the HK54. This early gun had a flip-type rear sight positioned forward over the magazine well. The barrel had cooling ribs and two lateral slots cut over the muzzle to serve as a compensator. The forearm had cooling slots cut into it, and the bolt carrier was longer and heavier than current models.

By 1966, the Heckler & Koch submachine gun had emerged pretty much as we know it today and was renamed the MP5. The muzzle brake and cooling ribs were eliminated, and three external lugs were placed near the muzzle to accommodate a blank firing device, flash hider, and grenade launchers of both the ballistite and bullet trap types. The rear sight was relocated to the aft portion of the receiver and became the rotary-aperture type associated with the H&K system in general.

Other countries have manufactured the MP5 under license from Heckler & Koch for domestic use only. These include POF of Pakistan, MKE of Turkey, and Saudi Arabia. Greece is apparently licensed for the MP5 but has never produced anything but lavish advertising brochures. Mexico will soon commence licensed series production of the MP5. Portugal, which manufactures the G3 rifle under license, has never applied for a license to produce the MP5. Licensees purchase a specific technical data package from H&K, and thus their products do not reflect the modifications and improvements made over time at Oberndorf-Neckar.

Receiver Marking

Since the late 1970s, Heckler & Koch has employed a simple letter code marked on the top of the receiver, the bottom left side of all magazines, and some components, to indicate the year of manufacture. Given that "A" signifies zero, "B" means "1" and so on up to "J," which stands for "9," it's easy to date any H&K weapon or magazine. For example, a receiver marked "IF" tells us that the firearm was produced in 1985.

Proof Mark – Six Proof Houses in Germany. **ULM is utilized by HK**

ULM	Berlin	Kiel	Hannover	Munich	Koln

HK Date Code:

A = 0	**B = 1**	**C = 2**	**D = 3**	**E = 4**
F = 5	**G = 6**	**H = 7**	**I = 8**	**K = 9**

J is reserved for Proof house and on HK parts not required to be proof tested, such as magazine housings.

Trigger Group Options

Available in several versions, but all are based on the Standard S-E-F mechanism.

    A. Standard S-E-F (stands for S – *Sicher* - SAFE, E – *Einselfeuer* – Single shot, F – *Feuerstoss* – Burst of Fire)
    B. Navy trigger (ambidextrous S-E-F) – NT
    C. 2-round burst (Safe-Semi-2 round-sustained) – (0125)
    D. 3-round burst (Safe-Semi-3 round-sustained) – (0135)
    E. SF (Safe-Fire) – (SF)
    F. 2-round only (Safe-Semi-2-round) – (012)
    G. 3-round only (Safe-Semi-3-round) – (013)

The weapon is SAFE when set on "0," "S" (safe), or a white bullet in a rectangular box with an "X" superimposed over it; the selector lever's spindle prevents all upward movement of the sear, and its nose cannot drop out of engagement with the hammer's notch.

When put on "1," "E" (*einzeln* = single), or a red bullet in a box, pulling the trigger will rotate the sear down and out of the hammer's notch. When the hammer rotates forward, the sear slips forward, and its end drops down off a fixed step. In recoil, the hammer is rotated back by the bolt carrier and catches the sear's nose, pushing it back in contact with the fixed step. After the bolt closes again, the auto sear releases the hammer, which is then held by the sear. Releasing the trigger allows the tail end of the sear to rise and move onto the fixed step. Pulling the trigger again will repeat the process.

When the selector lever is set to "F" (*Feuerstoss* = burst/full-auto) or seven red bullets in a long box open at the front end (implying infinity), its spindle allows the sear's tail to rise so high that the sear's nose does not engage the hammer notch at all. The hammer is thus held by the auto sear only. As soon as the bolt carrier moves completely forward the auto sear is released and the hammer set free.

Two and 3-shot burst controls are also available. They consist of an intricate ratchet-counting device fitted to the trigger mechanism, which holds the sear off the hammer until the allotted number of rounds have been fired. The device ensures that only the correct number of rounds are fired in a single burst, and any interruption commences a new count. After each burst, the trigger must be released to set the counter back to zero. Although the burst mechanism is reliable when maintained properly, it adds significantly to the number of parts in the trigger mechanism.

There are now four trigger units available for the MP5 series. All have housings fabricated from a two-piece synthetic molding. The standard "SEF" group provides safe, semi-auto, and full-auto positions with a selector lever on the left side only. Its pistol grip has finger swells, while the others do not but are flared at the bottom in the front to prevent the firing hand from slipping downward. The Navy group offers the same three positions but uses bullets rather than numbers or letters for markings and is ambidextrous (a selector lever on each side of the housing). There is also the ambidextrous, four-position, 3-shot burst group.

The MP5 SF (single fire) carbine's ambidextrous trigger group has only two settings and will fire only in semi-automatic. In addition, a special selector lever and lockout key are available to prevent the "SEF" trigger group from firing in the full-auto mode. The selector lever on all of these trigger groups can easily be pushed downward with the thumb of the firing hand while retaining the correct firing grip. However, the lever cannot be rotated upward – back to safe – without shifting the operator's grip. This remains as the single legitimate ergonomic criticism of the entire Heckler & Koch series.

Safety Operation

The safety lever on the trigger group has three positions.

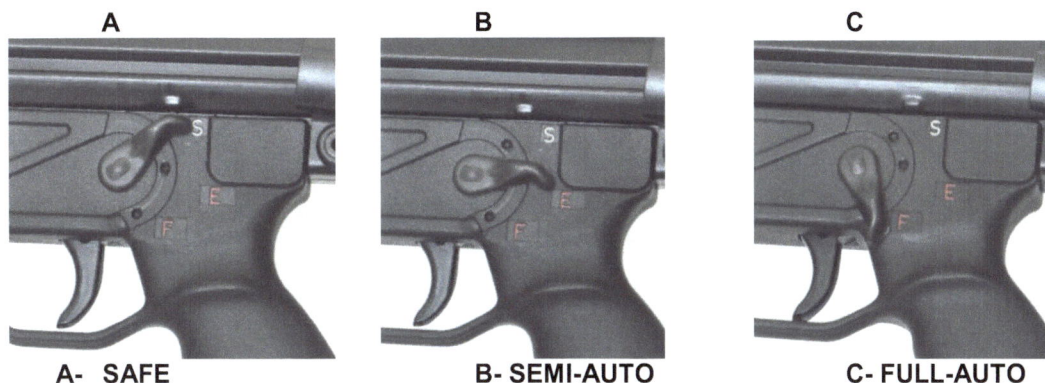

A	B	C
A- SAFE	B- SEMI-AUTO	C- FULL-AUTO

Figures 1-3 Photos of the selector lever in different positions

Sights

It should be noted that rotation of the rear sight on the MP5 will bring into view apertures of different diameters only. Elevation remains constant. Elevation adjustments are made by insertion of a special tool with two spring-loaded wedges into the rear sight cylinder, to engage two slots in the axis shaft that contain the spring-loaded catch bolts. When the catch bolts have been depressed, the sight cylinder can then be freely rotated around its threaded axis shaft in the desired direction. The tool also contains a Phillips-head screwdriver used to loosen the lock screw and turn the windage adjusting screw.

Once zero adjustments have been performed, there is little requirement for continued sight adjustment of a submachine gun. The well-protected front sight post is not adjustable. Best employed as a ghost ring, the largest rear aperture should be used at all times, except when engaging targets at longer ranges with semi-automatic fire. Self-luminous tritium front and rear sight inserts are available from H&K as an option.

Stock

All MP5 stocks, except those designed for the MP5K series, are interchangeable. Although the fixed buttstock provides the most stable firing platform and is to be preferred, the MP5's retractable stock is among the best of this type.

Magazines

HK MP5 magazines come in two capacities, 15- and 30-round and other capacities from non-HK aftermarket manufacturers. They are of the modern two-position feed type. They are well made entirely of steel, and the floor plate is held securely in place by two side tabs (although they are a bit more tedious to disassemble than more conventional designs). The original 30-round magazine was a straight, uncurved box with a plastic follower. Feed problems with some lots of ammunition encouraged a change in 1977 to a curved magazine with a chromed-steel follower.

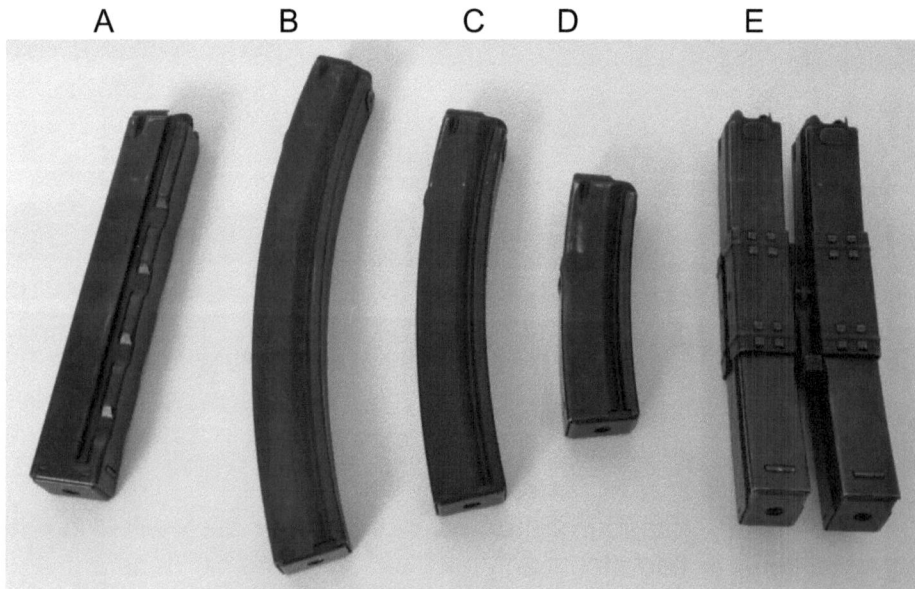

Figure 1-4 Photo of the different MP5 magazines
A- 30-round straight   B- 40-round   C- 30-round curved
D- 15-round   E. 2- 30-round with HK Mag coupler

A newly designed translucent 30-round magazine for the MP5/10 and MP5/40 allows the operator to see the immediate status of rounds remaining. These magazines snap together without the need of an accessory coupler clamp, in a manner reminiscent of the Swiss SG 550/551 assault rifles. These uncurved, straight box-type magazines are made from a specially developed high-strength polymer that makes them 30% lighter and impervious to corrosion.

Because of this weapon's closed-bolt method of operation, only 29 rounds should be loaded, as MP5 magazines stuffed with 30 rounds will not always seat in the magazine well if the bolt group is forward. Also, when the tactical situation permits, the operator should observe whether the top round was on the left or right of the staggered column prior to insertion and charging, and then remove the magazine to establish that the top round has moved over (indicating that round has been chambered).

Nomenclature

Figure 1-5 Photo of the overall MP5 SMG disassembled

1- Muzzle
2- Protected Front Sight
3- Cocking Handle
4- Magazine Well
5- Magazine Release Lever
6- Rear Sight
7- Endcap
8- Buttstock
9- Locking Pin
10- Guide Rod/Recoil Spring
11- Trigger Group
12- Bolt Carrier
13- Locking Piece, Firing Pin, and Spring
14- Bolt Head
15- Forearm
16- Locking Pin

Figure 1-6 MP5 trigger group

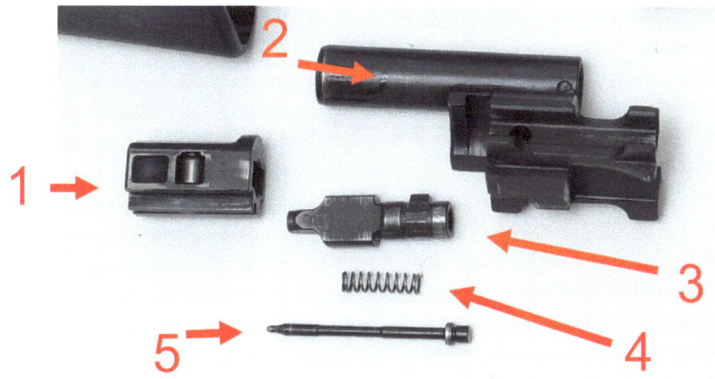

Figure 1-7 MP5 bolt carrier assembly pieces

1- Bolt Head	2- Bolt Carrier	3- Locking Piece
4- Firing Pin Spring	5- Firing Pin	

Variants

MAJOR VARIANTS TO THE MP5

3 Families of the MP5 A, SD, and K
A — *(950 RPM)*
SD — Schall Daempfer (Sound Damped) *(900 RPM)*
K — Kurz (Short) *(1100 RPM)*

MP5A Models- (There are an endless combinations, but these are the most common)
MP5A — Basic series submachine gun in 9x19mm introduced around 1965 with two new variations of the "A" in .40 S&W and 10mm introduced in 1993
MP5A1 - Submachine Gun with buttcap
MP5A2 - Submachine Gun with fixed stock
MP5A3 - Submachine Gun with retractable stock
MP5A4 - Submachine Gun with fixed stock
MP5A5 - Submachine Gun with retractable stock
MP5SFA2 - Single Fire Carbine/SMG with fixed stock
MP5SFA3 - Single Fire Carbine/SMG with retractable stock
MP5-N - SMG with retractable stock, Navy trigger, threaded muzzle, optional front sight, and optional stainless-steel suppressor
MP5/40 - SMG in caliber .40 S&W, bolt hold open feature, threaded muzzle
MP5/10 - SMG in 10mm, bolt hold open feature, threaded muzzle

MP5SD Models- (There are an endless combinations, but these are the most common.)
MP5SD — Second model introduced around 1970. The SD has an integral suppressor to reduce the velocity of standard ammunition to a subsonic level. It must not be fired without the suppressor. *Use Standard ammo – DON'T USE LEAD AMMUNITION – Bleeds off 200 feet per second/fps – Clean every 300 rounds*

MP5SD1 - Suppressed SMG with buttcap
MP5SD2 - Suppressed SMG with fixed stock
MP5SD3 - Suppressed SMG with retractable stock with Navy trigger group
MP5SD6 - Suppressed SMG with retractable stock with Navy trigger group

MP5K Models-
MP5K - Short SMG/adjustable sights
MP5KA1 - Short SMG/fixed sights
MP5KA4 - Short SMG/fixed sights

MP5K (w/bc)   - Short SMG/w/briefcase
MP5K (N)   - Short SMG/w/Navy trigger, threaded barrel, beta night
            sights, optional stainless-steel suppressor
MP5K (PDW)   - Short SMG with folding stock

Note: A2 and A4 are Fixed Stock and A3 and A5, Retractable Stock.

MP5A4

Figure 1-8 MP5A4

Caliber: 9x19 mm NATO

Type: Delayed blowback, closed bolt

Overall length: 67.5 cm/26.5 inches

Weight unloaded: 2.9 kg/6.4 pounds

Barrel length: 22.5 cm/8.85 inches

Magazine capacity: 30 detachable box magazine

Rate of Fire: 800 rounds per minute (rpm)

Maximum Effective Range: 200 meters

MP5A3

Figure 1-9 MP5A3

Caliber: 9x19mm NATO

Type: Delayed blowback, closed bolt

Overall length: 55 cm/21.6 inches – retracted stock; 69 cm/27 inches – extended stock

Weight unloaded: 3.1 kg/6.8 pounds

Barrel length: 22.5 cm/8.85 inches

Magazine capacity: 30 detachable box magazine

Rate of Fire: 800 rounds per minute (rpm)

Maximum Effective Range: 200 meters

MP5SD3

Figure 1-10 MP5SD3

Caliber: 9x19mm NATO

Type: Delayed blowback, closed bolt

Overall length: 66 cm/26 inches – retracted stock; 80 cm/31.4 inches – extended stock

Weight unloaded: 3.4 kg/7.5 pounds

Barrel length: 14.6 cm/5.7 inches

Magazine capacity: 30 detachable box magazine

Rate of Fire: 800 rounds per minute (rpm)

Maximum Effective Range: 200 meters

The MP5SD is the sound-suppressed version of the MP5. The barrel has been ported and surrounded by a tubular casing. Escaping gases are diverted through the barrel's ports to drop the bullet's velocity below the sonic level before it leaves the muzzle. The muzzle blast's sound level is drastically reduced by a helix within the casing, which increases the gas volume and decreases its temperature.

MP5K

Figure 1-11 MP5K

Caliber: 9x19mm NATO

Type: Delayed blowback, closed bolt

Overall length: 32 cm/12.5 inches

Weight unloaded: 2 kg/4.4 pounds

Barrel length: 11.5 cm/4.5 inches

Magazine capacity: 30 detachable box magazine

Rate of Fire: 900 rounds per minute (rpm)

Maximum Effective Range: 100 meters

Figure 1-12 MP5K with brief case

MP5SF

Figure 1-13 MP5SF

Caliber: 9x19mm NATO

Type: Delayed blowback, closed bolt, semi-automatic model

Overall length: 67.5 cm/26.5 inches

Weight unloaded: 2.9 kg/6.4 pounds

Barrel length: 22.5 cm/8.85 inches

Magazine capacity: 30 detachable box magazine

Rate of Fire: Single Shot

Maximum Effective Range: 200 meters

MP5N

Figure 1-14 MP5N

Caliber: 9x19mm NATO

Type: Delayed blowback, closed bolt

Overall length: 55 cm/21.6 inches – retracted stock; 69 cm/27 inches – extended stock

Weight unloaded: 3.1 kg/6.8 pounds

Barrel length: 22.5 cm/8.85 inches

Magazine capacity: 30 detachable box magazine

Rate of Fire: 800 rounds per minute (rpm)

Maximum Effective Range: 200 meters

MP5-PDW

Figure 1-15 MP5-PDW

Caliber: 9x19mm NATO

Type: Delayed blowback, closed bolt

Overall length: 33 cm/13 inches – retracted stock; 57 cm/22.4 inches – extended stock

Weight unloaded: 2.5 kg/5.5 pounds

Barrel length: 14.8 cm/5.8 inches

Magazine capacity: 30 detachable box magazine

Rate of Fire: 900 rounds per minute (rpm)

Maximum Effective Range: 100 meters

The MP5K-PDW (Personal Defense Weapon) combines the MP5K with the side-folding stock. The barrel has been extended to 5 inches so as to include the three mounting lugs and threads for the suppressor. With the stock and suppressor, the total weight empty is 7.4 pounds. Both shoulder and leg harnesses are available. It is intended to serve as a compact weapon for vehicle or aircraft crewmen, but has obvious applications for special operations.

MP5/10

Figure 1-16 MP5/10

Caliber: 10mm

Type: Delayed blowback, closed bolt

Overall length: 682 cm/26.8 inches (fixed stock)

Weight unloaded: 2.85 kg/6.2 pounds

Barrel length: 22 cm/8.7 inches

Magazine capacity: 30 detachable box magazine

Rate of Fire: 800 rounds per minute (rpm)

Maximum Effective Range: 100 meters

A spring-loaded, ribbed bolt catch (located on the left side of the receiver directly above the trigger pack) holds the MP5/10 and MP5/40 bolts to the rear after the last round is fired. Depressing the bolt-catch release lever permits the bolt group to travel forward and chamber the first round after a loaded magazine has been inserted.

There is the usual high degree of interchangeability of parts, accessories, stocks and slings between the MP5/10 and MP5/40 and 9x19mm MP5s. The 3-shot-burst trigger group is standard, but all of the other MP5 trigger groups are available as options.

MP5/40

Figure 1-17 MP5/40

Caliber: .40 Smith & Wesson

Type: Delayed blowback, closed bolt

Overall length: 68 cm/26.8 inches

Weight unloaded: 2.85 kg/6.2 pounds

Barrel length: 22.5 cm/8.8 inches

Magazine capacity: 30 detachable box magazine

Rate of Fire: 800 rounds per minute (rpm)

Maximum Effective Range: 70 meters

A spring-loaded, ribbed bolt catch (located on the left side of the receiver directly above the trigger pack) holds the MP5/10 and MP5/40 bolts to the rear after the last round is fired. Depressing the bolt-catch release lever permits the bolt group to travel forward and chamber the first round after a loaded magazine has been inserted.

There is the usual high degree of interchangeability of parts, accessories, stocks and slings between the MP5/10 and MP5/40 and 9x19mm MP5s. The 3-shot-burst trigger group is standard, but all of the other MP5 trigger groups are available as options.

Section 2

Maintenance

Figure 2-1 Photo of the overall MP5 SMG disassembled

1- Muzzle   2- Protected Front Sight   3- Cocking Handle
4- Magazine Well   5- Magazine Release Lever   6- Rear Sight
7- Endcap   8- Buttstock   9- Locking Pin
10- Guide Rod/Recoil Spring   11- Trigger Group   12- Bolt Carrier
13- Locking Piece, Firing Pin, and Spring   14- Bolt Head
15- Forearm   16- Locking Pin

Figure 2-2 MP5 trigger group

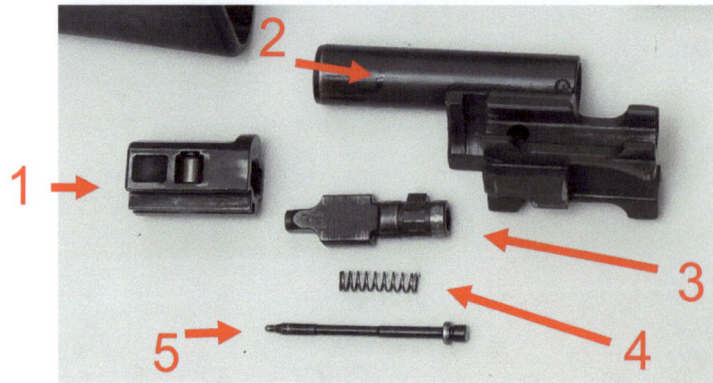

Figure 2-3 MP5 bolt carrier assembly pieces

1- Bolt Head   2- Bolt Carrier   3- Locking Piece
4- Firing Pin Spring   5- Firing Pin

Clearing the MP5 SMG

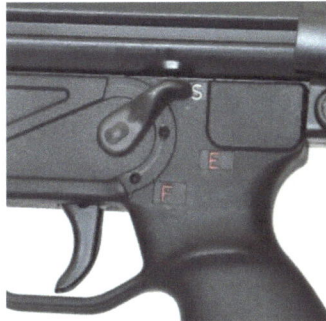

Figure 2-4 MP5 SMG Selector in the SAFE position

A. Ensure the SMG is on SAFE and pointed in a safe direction.

Figure 2-5a

Figure 2-5b

B. Remove the magazine by pressing the magazine release lever forward (Figure 2-5a) and pull the magazine from the magazine well (Figure 2-5b). Place the magazine in a pocket or magazine pouch or set it down.

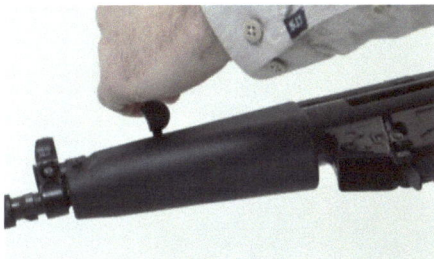

Figure 2-6a

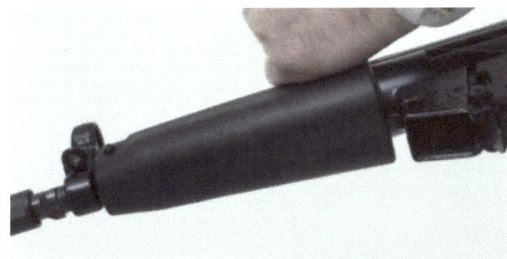

Figure 2-6b

C. Pull the cocking handle to the rear (Figure 2-6a) and up to lock the bolt to the rear (Figure 2-6b). Observe the round extracting and ejecting from the ejection port; do not attempt to retain the round.

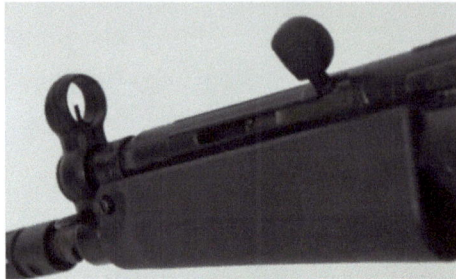
Figure 2-7a

Figure 2-7b

D. With the cocking handle locking the bolt into the open positon (Figure 2-7a), now visually check the chamber for a round (Figure 2-7b).

Figure 2-8

E. Once you have ensured the SMG has no magazine in it and the chamber is free of a round, you now can close the bolt by hitting the charging handle down to remove it from the locking notch (Figure 2-8).

Disassembling the MP5 SMG

NOTE- Place the SMG's parts on a flat, clean surface with the muzzle oriented in a safe direction.

When the operator begins to disassemble the pistol, it should be done in the following order:

Figure 2-9

A. Remove the locking pin in the rear of the receiver (Figure 2-9); place it in the stock holes or the hole it came from on the buttstock so it is not misplaced.

Figure 2-10

B. Remove the buttstock/butt cap (Figure 2-10).

Figure 2-11

C. Rotate the trigger assembly down and off the receiver (Figure 2-11).

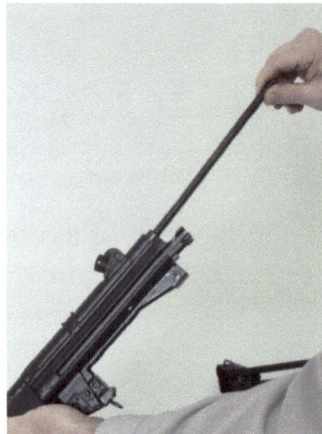
Figure 2-12

D. Remove the guide rod/recoil spring assembly (Figure 2-12).

Figure 2-13

E. Remove the bolt assembly (Figure 2-13), using the charging handle if necessary.

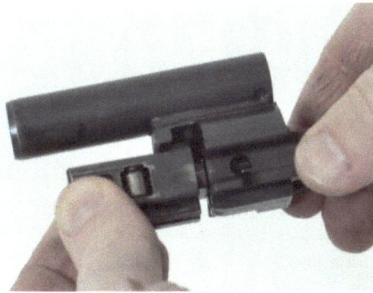

Figure 2-14

F. Slide the bolt head forward (Figure 2-14) until the top tabs meet and the rollers will retract into the bolt head.

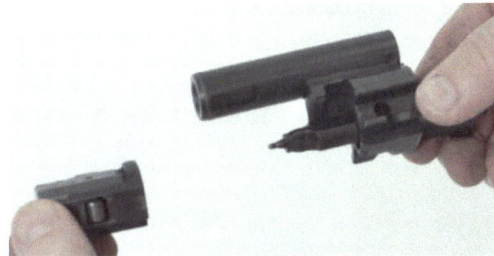

Figure 2-15a   **Figure 2-15b**

G. Rotate the bolt head just until the top tab clears (Figure 2-15a) and allow the bolt head to be slid forward off the locking piece (Figure 2-15b). If you rotate the bolt head too far to the right, the spring tension of the firing pin spring will eject the head off the carrier, if so, you are ahead.

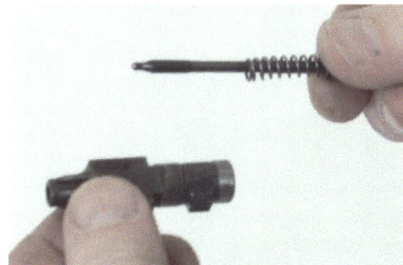

Figure 2-16a   **Figure 2-16b**

H. Rotate the locking piece cam lobe so that it is down and can be removed from the bolt carrier head (Figure 2-16a) and remove the firing pin and spring from the locking piece (Figure 2-16b).

LOCKING PIECE

The locking piece angles are critical to the proper function and safety of the gun; don't grind or stone on them. There are locking pieces for each of the variants.

They are marked as follows:

A	**=**	**NO MARKINGS** 8" barrel
SD	**=**	**5 or SD only** 6" barrel, #5 old marking
K	**=**	**16** 4" barrel
PDW	**=**	**80** 5" barrel
.40 cal =		**26** (old) **lo 24** (new)
10mm =		**24 Low impulse, 25 Hi impulse**

Do not interchange these locking pieces!

Figure 2-17a

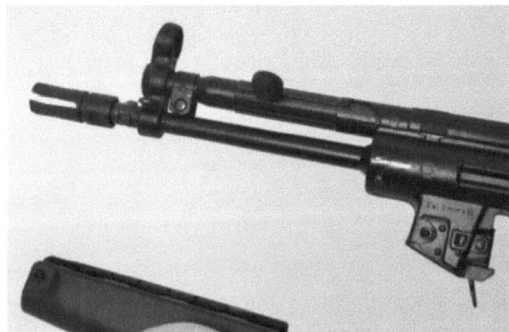

Figure 2-17b

I. Remove the locking pin (Figure 2-17a) and the handguard (Figure 2-17b) as needed; retain the pin back into the forearm.

Reassembling the MP5 SMG

Figure 2-18a

Figure 2-18b

A. Place the forearm back on the SMG if removed for disassembly (Figures 2-18a and 2-18b).

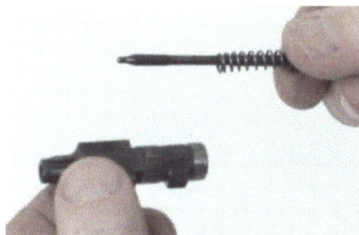
Figure 2-19

B. Reinsert the firing pin onto its spring (Figure 2-19) and into the locking piece.

Figure 2-20

C. Insert into the locking piece (Figure 2-20), oriented with the locking lobe down.

Figure 2-21

D. Place the locking piece with the firing pin and spring into the bolt carrier with the cam lobe down, press in, and slightly rotate it LEFT (Figure 2-21).

Figure 2-22a

Figure 2-22b

E. Place the bolt head onto the locking piece (Figure 2-22a) and rotate it into the locked position, LEFT (Figure 2-22b).

Figure 2-23

F. Place the guide rod/recoil spring assembly into the back of the bolt (Figure 2-23).

Figure 2-24

G. Orient the muzzle down and slide the bolt assembly into the receiver, bolt head first (Figure 2-24).

Figure 2-25a

Figure 2-25b

H. Place the front of the trigger assembly into the bottom notch on the receiver (Figure 2-25a) and rotate upwards (Figure 2-25b); ensure the hammer is cocked.

Figure 2-26

I. Remove the locking pin from the stock and place the stock/butt cap onto the rear of the receiver (Figure 2-26), retaining the trigger assembly.

Figure 2-27

J. Insert the locking pin into the end cap (Figure 2-27).

Performing a Function Check on the MP5 SMG

Ensure there is no magazine in the weapon; clear prior to performing a function check.

A. Pull the cocking handle to the rear and release. Ensure the selector lever is on SAFE and pull the trigger. The hammer should not fall.

B. Place the selector lever on SEMI. Pull the trigger and hold it to the rear. The hammer should fall.

C. Pull the cocking handle to the rear and release. Release the trigger, hear the reset, and pull again. The hammer should fall.

D. Pull the cocking handle to the rear and release. Place the selector lever on AUTO. Pull the trigger and hold it to the rear. The hammer should fall.

E. Pull the cocking handle to the rear several times and release. Release the trigger and pull again. The hammer should not fall.

F. Pull the cocking handle to the rear, release, and pull the trigger. The hammer should fall.

G. Pull the cocking handle to the rear and release. Place the selector lever on SAFE.

Maintenance of the Magazine

A. Disassembly
     a. Push the locking plate into the magazine housing.
     b. Press tabs in and remove the floor plate.
     c. Remove the follower spring, follower, and the locking plate.

When the magazine is disassembled, remove any dust, dirt, or foreign material from the magazine body and wipe off all the parts.

B. Assembly
     a. Insert the follower, magazine spring and the locking plate into the magazine body and push the locking plate into the magazine.
     b. Place the floor plate onto the magazine.

Section 3

Operation and Function

Cycle of Function
1. Feeding
2. Chambering
3. Locking
4. Firing
5. Unlocking
6. Extracting
7. Ejecting
8. Cocking

Loading the MP5 Magazine

NOTE- Ensure you have appropriate ammunition for the model to be used. Inspect it for uniformity, cleanliness, and serviceability. Check all cartridges for undented primers and only use issued ammunition.

1. Load cartridges into the magazine.

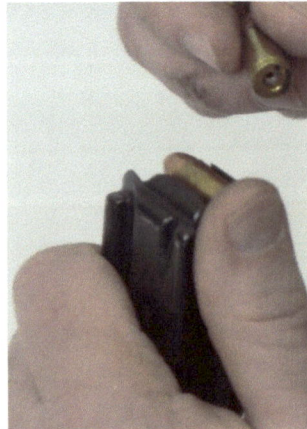 

Figure 3-1a   **Figure 3-1b**
Magazine hand-loading procedure

A. Use your non-dominant hand to hold the magazine with the front of the magazine toward your fingertips and your thumb as a guide on the rear of the magazine. With your dominant hand, one at a time, place the cartridge over the top of the magazine follower between the feed lips and press the cartridge straight down until it snaps under the feed lips. Once the cartridge is under the lip of the magazine body, slide it fully to the rear so the next round will be allowed to be pushed down (Figures 3-1a and 3-1b).

B. The magazine can hold 31 cartridges, but due to overloading of the spring, this should not be done; load 30 and then load the chamber so you have 29 in the magazine and one in the chamber and just 30 rounds in magazines you load for your pouches. The easiest approach is to lay out the number of rounds for each magazine so you don't have to count the rounds as you load the magazine.

Loading the magazine into a MP5 SMG

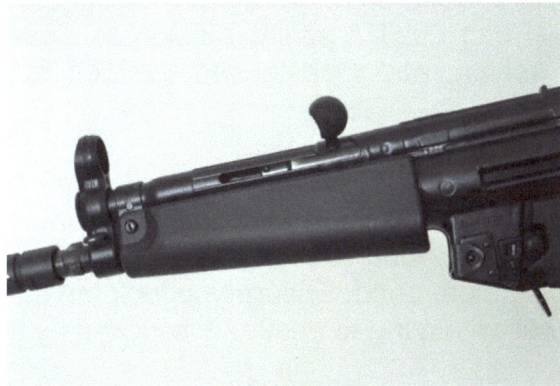

Figure 3-2

A. With the SMG pointed in a safe direction, on SAFE, and the bolt locked to the rear (Figure 3-2),

Figure 3-3a

Figure 3-3b

B. insert the loaded magazine into the magazine well (Figure 3-3a). Pull down on the magazine with the loading hand to ensure it is locked in by the magazine catch (Figure 3-3b).

Figure 3-4

C. Slap down onto the top of the cocking handle (Figure 3-4) while sliding into the down position so as to release it from the locking notch on the receiver, allowing the full spring tension to close the bolt. Listen for everything seating and look to see the bolt is fully forward and in battery.

D. To perform a press check, you can remove the magazine and see if the alternate bullet is at the top of the magazine. A loaded mag has a top right side round, and once you chamber a round, the mag will now have a top left side round. Ensure you lock the magazine back into the magazine well with a tug to ensure it is locked by the magazine catch.

Firing the MP5 SMG

A. Orient downrange or towards the threat.

B. Rotate the safety lever down to the desired mode of fire with a thumb.

Figure 3-5 MP5 Sight alignment

C. As you orient your sights onto the target, press the trigger straight back so as not to interrupt the sight alignment with the sight picture (Figure 3-5). If firing single shots, release the trigger only forward enough to reset the trigger, and then press it straight to the rear if another shot is needed. If firing full automatic, practice how long you hold the trigger for the desired burst and the recoil management required to keep the group on the desired target.

D. When you have completed firing the SMG, place the safety lever into the SAFE (up) position.

Section 4

Performance Problems

Malfunction and Immediate Action Procedures

Malfunctions are usually preventable through good practices, but they may still occur out of the blue from time to time. Of course, you hope it is on the practice range, but you should treat each one as though you are in a life-or-death situation. Practicing proper and effective corrective actions will allow you to be more confident in your weapon handling. In stressful situations, you can become much more stressed due to an unforeseen malfunction that is easy to correct. I have observed many shooters that perceive themselves to be experienced, but when they encounter a stovepipe, they nearly disassemble the weapon rather than sweep it out and continue.

Malfunction drills must fix the problem 100% of the time (excluding a weapon stoppage — broken weapon) the first time performed. You must look at the SMG and identify the problem (obviously the SMG is not functioning as you need, so you must transition to another weapon or rectify the situation). It is a non-functioning weapon at this point — fix it.

You should always practice taking a covered position to correct malfunctions with considerations on how you operate.

The following pages in this chapter describe and detail corrective actions for the various malfunctions that may be encountered.

MALFUNCTION	CAUSE	CORRECTION
1. Failure to Feed	Magazine – Dirty	Clean
	- Dented	Replace
	- Lips Bent	Replace
	- Spring Broken	Replace spring
	- Loaded Wrong	Reload
	- Not Seated	Reseat
	Recoil Spring Broken/Bent	Replace
	Weapon Dirty	Clean
2. Failure to Chamber	Chamber Fouled	Clean
	Barrel Extension Fouled	Clean
	Deformed Cartridge	Pull back cocking handle and rechamber
	Weak or Broken Recoil Spring	Replace
	Receiver Bent	Replace
3. Failure to Lock	Missing Rollers	Inspect for damage Replace rollers
4. Failure to Fire	Firing Pin or Spring Broken	Replace
	Bolt not fully Locked	Recock and attempt to fire
5. Failure to Extract	Chamber Fouled	Clean
	Extractor Broken	Clean
6. Failure to Eject	Extractor/Ext. Spring Broken	Replace
	Extractor Spring Weak	Replace
	Ejector Broken	Replace
7. Failure to Cock	Hammer Broken	Replace
8. Recoil Hard	Bolt Carrier Striking Back Plate	Replace Buffer

FAILURE-TO-GO-INTO BATTERY:

NOTE: The <u>failure-to-go-into-battery malfunction</u>, when your bolt assembly does not fully return forward when cycling a round, is always rectified in the same manner. This malfunction is usually induced when loading and not allowing the full recoil spring tension to shut the slide.

To fix a failure-to-go-into-battery malfunction, you must ensure your finger is off the trigger and outside the triggerguard, and then rotate the SMG to the right (ejection port to ground). Then pull the cocking handle to the rear with the non-firing hand. Let the round fall to the ground, and once the cocking handle is fully to the rear, release it to close by its own spring tension. Listen and look for it fully seating the next round from the magazine.

FAILURE TO FIRE: This malfunction occurs when the operator has loaded a dud cartridge or failed to load the chamber. The universal fix all for this is the "<u>Slap</u>, <u>Rack</u>, <u>Bang</u>" technique.

SYMPTOM - You perform a full presentation to shoot and hear and feel the hammer strike, and the weapon does not fire.

CORRECTION:

1. **<u>SLAP</u>** – the bottom of the magazine with a hard palm (fingers extended) to ensure it is fully seated and locked in.

2. **<u>RACK</u>** – the cocking handle fully to the rear and release it to shut by its own recoil spring tension. You can pivot the SMG toward your non-firing hand to assist in racking the cocking handle to the rear; maintain muzzle to threat orientation.

3. **<u>BANG</u>** – or represent and prepare to fire the shot as you intended before the malfunction if your situation dictates that action.

FAILURE TO EJECT: This malfunction (commonly called a "stovepipe") is usually created by the bolt being retarded in its rearward movement to rechamber the next round or a weak extractor spring. This malfunction is easily corrected by ejecting the expended case from the port by turning the SMG ejection port to the ground and cycling the action.

SYMPTOM - You are in the act of shooting a multiple-round engagement, and you notice you felt the bolt assembly did not fully close, and/or have a soft, mushy trigger.

CORRECTION:
With the non-firing hand, extend your fingers, and with fingers joined, reach for the cocking handle. (DO NOT SWEEP YOUR HAND IN FRONT OF THE MUZZLE.) Roll your fingers around the cocking handle and with a firm, vigorous

sweeping motion to the rear, pull the cocking handle to the rear while orienting the ejection port to the ground. Roll the SMG left and look into the ejection port, and there should be no loose rounds. If there is a round in the magazine (if not, reload or transition to your pistol), release the cocking handle to close on its own spring tension and reorient to the threat.

Once the casing is no longer pinched by the bolt, the release of the cocking handle will continue to seat the next round, and you are now ready to continue the engagement. Many inexperienced shooters do too much to correct this simple malfunction.

FAILURE TO EXTRACT: This malfunction (commonly called a "double feed") is created when the spent casing is not extracted from the chamber (may be due to a damaged extractor or weak extractor spring), and the next round to be loaded is rammed from the magazine into the rear of the stuck casing. This malfunction is a serious one since more complicated dexterity is needed to correct it and, of course, to do it quickly. Below is the breakdown of the corrective action to restore your pistol back to operation.

SYMPTOM - You are shooting a multiple-shot engagement and notice your slide did not go forward; you have a soft, mushy trigger; and it will not fire.

CORRECTION:
STEP ONE – With the non-firing hand, extend your fingers, and with fingers joined, reach for the cocking handle. (DO NOT SWEEP YOUR HAND IN FRONT OF THE MUZZLE.) Roll your fingers around the cocking handle, and with a firm, vigorous sweeping motion to the rear, pull the cocking handle to the rear while orienting the ejection port to the ground. Roll the SMG to the left and look into the ejection port and there should be no loose rounds. If there is a round in the magazine and not loose round/cases, just release the cocking handle to close on its own spring tension and reorient to the threat. If a round is present, move to the next step.

STEP TWO – Lock the bolt to the rear and remove the magazine from the SMG.

STEP THREE – Rack the bolt to the rear at least two times to ensure the casing is extracted and ejected from the SMG. As you are doing this step, observe the casing being ejected and allow the action to use its spring tension to shut each time it is pulled to the rear.

STEP FOUR – Properly insert and seat a loaded magazine.

STEP FIVE – Hit the cocking handle down to release it to close by its own spring tension. Your SMG is now ready to continue the engagement.

STEP SIX – Continue the engagement as the situation dictates.

NOTE: Correcting this malfunction needs to be practiced often since it is the most complicated to do under stress or when you lose dexterity because blood is leaving the extremities.